Youth Questions Answered

AF344277

Youth Questions Answered

by
Lee Fisher

BEACON HILL PRESS OF KANSAS CITY
Kansas City, Missouri

First printing, 1981
Beacon Hill Press of Kansas City
ISBN: 0-8341-0719-8

Printed in the
United States of America

The material in this book was previously printed in the *War Cry, U.S.A.* and is copyrighted by The Salvation Army. Permission has been granted to compile the articles and reprint in book form.

Unless otherwise indicated all Scripture quotations are taken from *The Holy Bible, New International Version* (NIV), copyright © 1978 by the New York International Bible Society, and are used by permission.

Cover design: Royce Ratcliff

Contents

Q: **When someone is angry and he speaks harshly to you, is he saying what he really feels?**—*P. R.*

A: Most of the time, P. R., when people "blow their top" and say things in anger, they are victims of hidden feelings which are not directly connected with their present situation. Their statements are usually exaggerations of some relatively minor grievance which is blown all out of proportion by anger. Frequently they feel sorry for what they have said, and realize their distorted thinking and feeling.

In other words, when people have numerous frustrations in one or more areas of their lives which they cannot resolve or refuse to face, they subconsciously look for a scapegoat. Anger builds up like steam in a boiler, and they release or displace it on some relatively innocent person or situation.

There are some people who feel that if you get people angry, they will tell you the truth. However, this is not ordinarily the case. What they say are usually half-truths motivated by feelings other than love. They are actually blinded by anger and thus blind to the whole truth.

You have probably heard it said about someone that "he was so mad he couldn't see straight." This is often a psychologically sound explanation of outbursts of anger. What the person says is really dictated by the "logic of the emotions" rather than fact and reason. There is a temporary loss of intellectual control, and emotional feelings take over. There may be a limited amount of truth expressed, but it is usually too colored by the strong emotion of anger for you to take it seriously.

Also, when someone is angry and speaks harshly to you, he or she may be consciously or subconsciously trying to hurt you. If this is the case, his statements are aimed at your sensitive spots rather than the truth.

It is my feeling, P. R., that you can help an angry person by responding with love and understanding.

Q: **Did Jesus show any outward expression of violence while here on earth?—*M. G.***

A: There are two major meanings of violence, M. G., and in answering your question it is necessary that differences in definition be clarified. One common meaning of violence relates to the type of assault that is expressed in burglaries or thefts where someone is physically hurt or killed. This kind of assault occurs frequently in our society and is one of our unlawful social problems. On the other hand, the other definition of violence involves "strength or energy actively displayed or exerted," but without being unlawful. It is the kind of expression designed to change existing conditions, but motivated by holy desires and exercised in the process of defending the standards and principles of God, along with the legitimate rights of others.

In line with this second definition, there is evidence in the Scriptures that Jesus did show violence while here on earth. The Bible says, "In the temple courts he found men selling cattle, sheep and doves, and others sitting at tables exchanging money. So he made a whip out of cords, and drove all from the temple area, both sheep and cattle; he scattered the coins of the money changers and overturned their tables. To those who sold doves he said, 'Get these out of here! How dare you turn my Father's house into a market!'" (John 2:14-16). Jesus is usually portrayed as being only meek and mild, and sometimes people forget that He was so zealous for righteousness that He did not hesitate to outwardly display anger, even with physical force. He made it clear that meekness is not weakness, that real love for others and for His Heavenly Father does not create spineless and whimpering people.

However, please notice that Christ's anger was always expressed when the welfare of others, not himself, was at stake. When people spit upon Him personally, beat Him, and nailed Him to a cross, He did not get angry but was "led like a lamb to the slaughter" (Isaiah 53:7).

His anger and violence was a "righteous indignation" that expressed itself for others. Carnal anger is motivated by selfishness, but holy anger is designed to reach out and change unholy conditions. When you become a Christian, God does not take the ability to get angry out of you, but He helps you to direct it toward holy ends.

Q: **When is Jesus coming again?**—*Anonymous.*

A: The best answer to this can be summed up in the words of Jesus: "No one knows about that day or hour, not even the angels in heaven, nor the Son, but only the Father. Be on guard! Be alert! You do not know when that time will come" (Mark 13:32-33).

Although no one can predict the time of Christ's return, never doubt that He is coming again. There are 318 explicit references in the Bible to the second coming of Jesus. Since there are 1,189 chapters in the Scriptures, this averages out to about one reference for every three and three-fourths chapters. As important as the first coming of Christ is, you will probably be surprised to know that eight times more space is given to the Second Coming than to the first. About one-third of the Bible is prophecy, and of this amount approximately one-third is about Christ's return.

Many of the writers in the Bible spoke of this glorious event. Representative of these are 1 Peter 5:4; 2 Timothy 4:1 (Paul); and 1 John 3:1-3.

There are certain characteristics of His coming. It will be *personal* ("This same Jesus," Acts 1:11), and it will be *visible* ("every eye will see him," Revelation 1:7).

Although the Bible does not give a precise time of Christ's second coming, there are many signs that will point to His return—social, natural, moral, spiritual, and supernatural signs. Space prevents a detailed analysis here, but you will find these five areas covered in a good reference Bible.

When Christ comes again, He will come as a Bridegroom to take to himself His Bride, the Church or born-again believers. It will be a time of reunion (1 Thessalonians 4:16-17), reward (Revelation 22:12), and freedom from sickness and pain (Philippians 3:20-21), and Christ shall "reign for ever and ever" (Revelation 11:15).

Yes, Jesus is coming again! The time of His return is under His control, but let us "watch and pray" and be ready to meet Him if His literal return should be in our lifetime.

Q: **What should a Christian do when confronted by the cults?—*Anonymous*.**

A: First of all, don't develop an excessive curiosity about the cults. The dictionary defines a cult as a "great devotion to some person, idea, or thing, especially such devotion viewed as an intellectual fad." It is a well-known psychological fact that what gets your attention gets you! It is alright to understand what the various cults believe, and give your witness; but in the process don't spend so much time and effort analyzing the cults that you gradually get away from your Christian truth and doctrine.

Next, always remember that the cults are full of half-truths and do not preach the whole gospel. Their teachings will be presented to you as a special message from God by leaders or teachers who have been deluded into thinking that their message is divine.

The Bible says, "Dear friends, do not believe every spirit, but test the spirits to see whether they are from God, because many false prophets have gone out into the world" (1 John 4:1).

The real test for a Christian is whether Christ is at the center of his worship and beliefs. He is the divine Son of God, and thus all truth and gospel comes from His life and teachings as recorded in the Scriptures. This includes believing in the Trinity of God the Father, Son, and Holy Spirit. Cults may believe and quote some of the Bible, but their mainstream of emphasis actually leads people away from Christ into strange doctrines and beliefs.

When you are confronted by the cults, the best approach is to give your personal testimony and hold them to the Word of God. However, don't become involved in endless arguments, and don't become discouraged if you find it difficult to convert them to Christ. Their devotion to half-truths, strange doctrines, and false teachings have made them spiritually blind.

Your responsibility is to preach "Jesus Christ and him crucified" (1 Corinthians 2:2). "See to it that no one takes you captive through hollow and deceptive philosophy, which depends on human tradition and the basic principles of this world rather than on Christ" (Colossians 2:8).

Q: **Do you see any future in the increasing focus on spiritualistic or psychic phenomena? Is this something of the devil? —C. S.**

A: In answering your question, C. S., it is necessary to make a distinction between the scientific research in the area of psychic or mental activity which is within the legitimate scope of psychological studies, and the spiritualistic type of emphasis which is in the province of the occult. For example, Duke University for many years has done considerable scientific research in ESP (extrasensory perception). When psychologists were surveyed about 20 years ago, the majority did not even recognize the existence of such phenomena. However, more recent surveys indicate that more and more professional people consider it a "likely possibility."

Dr. Frank Laubach wrote a book entitled *Prayer* which included many references to study in ESP and advocated that people could be induced to pray to God more by having their minds influenced through the bombardment of ideas about God emanating from those who supposedly have ESP powers. Before his

SPRINGDALE CHURCH OF THE NAZARENE
11177 SPRINGFIELD PIKE
CINCINNATI, OHIO 45246

death his interest in this approach waned considerably, and the scientific evidence did not support the confidence he had placed in these psychic powers.

A considerable number of experiments are in process by respectable scientists today which seek to enhance knowledge in this realm. The results thus far, however, are not of sufficient quality and quantity to seriously affect our understanding of human or spiritual nature.

Unfortunately, today the more popular and dangerous "discoveries" are in the realm of the occult and are of the devil. Witchcraft, for example, is growing at an alarming rate around the world. But it is a hoax, and its future can be nothing but ominous, blasphemous, and evil.

Nevertheless, there is actually a great scope for evangelism in the attention and focus placed upon spiritualistic and psychic phenomena. This scope lies in the recognition of a universal need and searching for the supernatural. Man was made in the image of God and hence has a soul and ability to relate to the spiritual world. The more Christians realize the universal vacuum of genuine spiritual life and reality, the more they will preach Christ, witness to their own spiritual relationship to Him, and emphasize the supernatural work of the Holy Spirit. This is a golden age for Christians to capitalize upon interest in the spiritual and psychic world and relate it to God through Jesus Christ. "God is spirit, and his worshipers must worship in spirit and in truth" (John 4:24).

Q: Please explain T.M. and why people get involved with this rather than with concentrating on God and His Word.—*V., Maine.*

A: Transcendental Meditation, or T.M., is a meditational technique which is used to gain relaxation and to heighten intellectual powers.

T.M. involves two 20-minute periods of meditation each day in which the person closes his eyes and concentrates upon his own privately assigned "mantra," which may be a nonsensical word, syllable, or sound. This is done to clear the mind of all other thoughts and to bring about a different level of consciousness.

T.M. was begun by the Hindu Maharishi Mahesh Yogi in 1958. His purpose was to "rechannel the course of humanity" by offering a "scientific technique" for the promotion of health and happiness.

Theologically, views held by T.M. are in contradiction to Christianity, as is the allegiance to Maharishi Mahesh Yogi instead of allegiance to Jesus Christ. The emphasis in T.M. is on self-justification by means of purposeful meditation as compared to the biblical method of justification by grace through faith.

Basically, T.M. may be a dangerous exercise, both mentally and spiritually, for it can be an escape from reality. In addition, the person may actually open himself to the influence of satanic powers.

Most people who practice T.M. have never experienced the liberating love of Christ, nor have they discovered the biblical ways to peace, joy, freedom, and creativity.

Christians should become increasingly aware of the tremendous resources available to them through the meditation of their hearts and minds upon God. There is no substitute for meditation on Jesus Christ through the divine revelation of the Holy Spirit.

DEATH

Q: Is suicide a sin?—*J. R.*

A: Your question is certainly timely, J. R. Suicide now is second only to accidents as the cause of death of those between 15 and 24 years of age, and is a serious personal, social, moral, and spiritual problem.

The sinfulness of suicide is best covered through understanding its relation to scriptural principles and the law of love. Failure to adhere to these is indication of committed sin.

The Bible teaches that God is sovereign or supreme in power and authority. Suicide attempts to usurp God in the realm of life and death, "playing God" by taking one's life in one's own hands. Only God has this authority. In addition, suicide shows ingratitude to God for the gift of life and says that God is inadequate to supply our needs, even when things may only temporarily look hopeless. This does not evidence living by faith in God.

Jesus taught that only those who do the will of God can enter heaven (Matthew 7:21-23). Suicide short-circuits God's will for a person's life by indirect disobedience. Nowhere does God's Word even remotely suggest that killing oneself is condoned by God or is part of His plan for mankind. When one ends his own life, he takes himself out of God's will, and this is sin.

Man ought to glorify God in everything (1 Corinthians 10:31). Suicide in no way glorifies God, as we are stewards accountable for the life He has given us.

Finally, Christ's law of love says, "Love each other as I have loved you" (John 15:12). Killing oneself is a selfish means of getting out of circumstances regardless of how it affects God or man and is not loving "as I have loved you."

Yes, suicide is sin, and you should do all you can to keep people from committing it. Faith in God works miracles, even in life's darkest hours!

Q: **What do you think of the current trend of books and movies on the subject of life after death? Do you consider them to be accurate?—*S. M.***

A: As I understand the current preoccupation with the subject of life after death, it is another projection of the deep need in man to understand and contact the supernatural, or forces beyond the natural world. Also, it reveals the need to establish hope for the future, give continuity between life and death, and to bring about a deeper sense of security. Of course, some of the writers and producers themselves may not be caught up in this subject due to their own personal interests. However, they know the needs, fears, hopes, and dreams of the majority of people, and they tailor their productions to sell. It becomes for many of them a matter of merchandising the "supernatural."

As you have probably already noted, there is a strong trend today in the matter of life and death to take God out of the whole process and reduce it to an extension of scientific research as a part of the natural world. Thus far, however, this endeavor has become a pseudoscience. That is, the research is unscientific and anecdotal or based on isolated incidents which are more like legends and myths than fact. The conclusions are incomplete, deceptive, and inaccurate.

They are fictional and not factual, and imaginative rather than realistic.

Let's face it, S. M., God does not intend for man through his own efforts to uncover the mystery of life after death. This is a divine *revelation*. God's Word is the best and only reliable source of information about the hereafter. In speaking about life after death, the Bible says, "Listen, I tell you a *mystery*" (1 Corinthians 15:51, italics added throughout). There are some things that God intends for man to know about death, and these are in the Word of God. The rest is a mystery, and to go beyond the Scriptures in this respect is mere speculation.

For those who are insecure, fearful, and without hope, may I suggest you have them read 1 Corinthians 15:51-58. For the Christian, there is no "sting" in death, but it is a time of "victory through our Lord Jesus Christ." Don't let a morbid curiosity, either in yourself or others, fabricate false ideas about life after death and thereby minimize God's divine revelation of this mystery.

Q: **What are some things that could help strengthen a Christian young person in a non-Christian home?**—*C. L.*

A: In order to strengthen your Christian experience in your home, C. L., there are at least three areas of your life that need special attention. That is, there are *three great sources of strength* from which you can receive help.

First of all, you need to continue to look for *upward support from God.* It is very easy for a Christian to become discouraged and confused by the everyday circumstances around his life. The Bible gives many examples of people who let their environment control their relationship to God.

Even though you find it necessary to read your Bible and pray in the secret of your own room, do not give up this source of strength. There is no substitute in the life of a Christian for the power of the Holy Spirit. When you "keep in step with the Spirit" and establish a good relationship with God, you will be strengthened (Galatians 5:25).

Second, you need *support from without.* During the early life of the Church, when Christians endured resistance and even persecution, they often met together to share their experience and to worship God. You need to continue to be faithful to your church and become involved with other young people who are Christians.

Finally, you need special *strength from within your own personality.* That is, you need to keep free from resentments, bitterness, and a judgmental attitude toward the rest of your family. Be obedient to your parents, accept and love those who even may criticize you, and keep a good spirit toward all.

One of the greatest inner strengths a person can have is a clear conscience. Learn to forgive and be kind to those who do not agree with you. As you receive power from your upward relationship with God, support from Christians outside your family, and keep a clear conscience and loving spirit within yourself, you will become strong in the Lord! (See Ephesians 3:14-21.)

Q: **What happens to a family when its members continue to disagree all the time and feelings keep building up?— *T. M.***

A: When conflicts are not satisfactorily solved in a family, one of the first casualties is an almost total *lack of communication.* When people cannot share both their thoughts and feelings with each other, they lose a sense of belonging, security, and trust.

Without communication there follows the *lack of understanding.* To be misunderstood leaves a feeling of isolation, rejection, and loneliness. There is something hopeless about "being on an island" socially, with little chance of escape.

Perhaps the most damaging effect of all is the build-up of hidden *feelings of bitterness and resentment,* which makes it impossible to love deeply and sincerely. A family without love is unhappy, uncooperative, and unholy.

What is needed, T. M., in a family like the one you have described is for someone to break through the logjam of misunderstanding, bitterness, and lack of communication by saying, "I'm sorry." This does not necessarily mean to intellectually agree with everything, but to admit sorrow for feelings of resentment or bitterness which have developed.

In my experience as a Christian psychologist I have seen many families united when just one member was willing to admit he or she was wrong in holding resentments, and then being willing to forgive. To forgive takes humility; proud people stay bitter and unforgiving.

No one is infallible but God. As long as humans have imperfect minds, they will never be able to agree on everything. However, they can "agree to disagree" in love and live as one happy family.

Q: **Should God be the Center of our family? It is my opinion that the family should come first, and this would bring a stronger relationship with God.—D. W.**

A: The encouraging aspect of your question, D. W., is that you have such a genuine respect and love for your family. There are so many people today who do not take family life seriously. This casual attitude fails to develop deep loyalties and abiding love. For them the family merely exists for convenience and social conformity rather than for mutual love.

The whole concept of the family has a divine origin. From the very beginning "God created man in his own image, in the image of God he created him; male and female he created them. God blessed them and said to them, 'Be fruitful and increase in number; fill the earth and subdue it'" (Genesis 1:27-28). The whole Bible supports God's plan to enhance and preserve family life. In fact, when a person becomes a Christian, he is adopted into the family of God: "Those who are led by the Spirit of God are sons of God. . . . you received the Spirit of sonship. And by him we cry, *'Abba,* Father'" (Romans 8:14-15).

These statements about God's high regard for the family concept, both human and divine, are intended to support your confidence in the family. It would thus be unscriptural for me to minimize the importance of the family and the need to love each member.

Nevertheless, insofar as our human families are concerned, the Bible does not support your opinion that the family should come first and God second. Jesus was very clear at this point and taught that God should be the Center of the family and all love relationships. Jesus said, "Anyone who loves his father or mother more than me is not worthy of me; anyone who loves his son or daughter more than me is not worthy of me" (Matthew 10:37). There are different directions and degrees of love, D. W., and Jesus makes it clear that God should be loved first.

When Christ is the Center of the family, the human love that each member has for one another is reinforced by divine love. When "God has poured out his love into our hearts" (Romans 5:5), we are not only better as a human family, but become a part of the family of God with a divine and eternal relationship. This can happen only when God is at the center.

Q: **Who is God?**

A: Perhaps the best way to answer is to first clarify who God is *not!* First of all, God is not just an *idea* formulated in the mind. He does not exist merely because we can think about Him. Neither does the nature of God depend upon the reasons the mind may give as to why He exists. God is bigger than the ideas and reasons that are used to explain Him.

Next, God is not the sum total of His *attributes*. The Bible ascribes many, many characteristics to God, but descriptions about God cannot substitute for God himself. God is love, mercy, righteousness, holiness, power, and scores of other marvelous things, but He cannot be understood merely by adding up His attributes.

In addition, God is not just a *name*. Certainly the Bible is careful to describe God through names, such as Jehovah and many others. However, to identify God's existence through names is substituting verbal symbols for the reality of God. When Moses asked God what name he should use when he came to the children of Israel to tell them that God had sent him, "God said to Moses, 'I am who I am. This is what you are to say to the Israelites: "I AM has sent me to you"'"

(Exodus 3:14). God did not want to be limited by a name.

But in considering who God *is,* the Bible says, "God is *spirit,* and his worshipers must worship in spirit and in truth" (John 4:24). The apostle Paul said, "This is what we speak, not in words taught us by human wisdom but in words taught by the Spirit, expressing spiritual truths in spiritual words" (1 Corinthians 2:13). Only the spirit of man as it comes in contact with the Holy Spirit can really know who God is. The Scriptures make it clear that God can only truly be known through divine revelation in the realm of the Spirit.

Second, God is a *person.* The apostle Paul said, "I know whom I have believed" (2 Timothy 1:12). The personal pronoun "whom" points up that God is not just an abstract force or an impersonal power. Anyone who wants to know God must seek a personal relationship with Him. The emphasis must be in the area of personal experience and not just intellectual comprehension.

Finally, *Jesus Christ* is God! The Bible says, "The Word became flesh and lived for a while among us" (John 1:14). The Scripture says, "God was reconciling the world to himself in Christ" (2 Corinthians 5:19). To know Jesus Christ is to know who God is. The Bible tells us about God, but it also tells us how we may know who He is personally through Jesus.

Q: Why does God let a handicapped or retarded person be born?—*D. I.*

A: When Jesus passed by and saw a man who had been blind from birth and was asked by His disciples if the blindness was due to sin, He replied, "Neither this man nor his parents sinned, . . . but this happened so that the work of God might be displayed in his life" (John 9:3). The answer as to why the man was born blind clearly states that God had a purpose in letting it happen. It is often impossible for man to discern the reason why God, in His permissive will, allows things to happen which appear through human eyes to be tragedies.

In the case of the blind man, the "works of God" were to heal him and thus demonstrate immediate supernatural power. This is not always God's purpose in allowing people to be born blind or with some other physical or mental problem. However, there is no question that what man often views as a tragedy is actually, from the divine perspective, a blessing. The problem is usually the difficulty man has in knowing and accepting God's purposes and seeing the positive side of what happens. This is true, for example, of the crucifixion of our Lord. Unless one sees God's purpose in allowing Jesus to suffer and die to pay the penalty for man's sin, the whole experience pictures

God as cruel, impersonal, and indifferent to the suffering and humiliation of His Son. But the "works of God" on the Cross are redemptive for all men when they accept this salvation and believe in God's plan of redemption.

The Bible says, "None of us lives to himself alone and none of us dies to himself alone" (Romans 14:7). That is, through both life and death we all have an influence upon someone. Who but God is to judge the ultimate influence for good of a handicapped or retarded person? No doubt most people reading this article can immediately think of someone in these conditions who has been a blessing to them, taught them lessons about life, become genuine objects of their love, or stimulated praise and thanksgiving to God for their own good health and strength.

May I suggest, D. I., that you resist the temptation to second-guess God. He brings victory through defeat, redemption through suffering, and blessing out of what you may view as tragedy. God is a God of love and eternal purpose. He alone knows the ultimate reason for it all!

Q: I'm a born-again Christian, but I have a struggle with my strong will and God's will for me. What can I do?—*C. C.*

A: There is a difference in being saved from sin and saved from self. A born-again Christian has been forgiven of committed sins; the guilt is gone because Christ paid sin's penalty on the Cross.

Still, the Bible clearly distinguishes between babies in Christ and mature Christians with desires committed wholly to God. The Corinthians were admonished by God through Paul who wrote, "Brothers, I could not address you as spiritual but as worldly—mere infants in Christ. I gave you milk, not solid food, for you were not yet ready for it. Indeed, you are still not ready. You are still worldly" (1 Corinthians 3:1-3).

There is a difference between confession of sin and consecration of the will. True confession leads to genuine repentance of sinful acts and determination never to repeat them. Consecration leads to full surrender and a willingness to obey God in everything. Your struggle's main source, C. C., is in not yielding your will to God's will. You still determine to have your own way and follow your own desires.

It is not a sin to have a strong will. In fact, strong-willed people are loyal to their convictions and able to maintain them. Willpower is a mighty force but needs to be harnessed, for it is a sin not to let your will be disciplined by God's will.

Also, take a long look at who God really is. Your God may be "too small" if you do not see and accept God as God. In comparing your limited knowledge with His, you should see the need to abdicate the throne of your life to Him. Much of your struggle is produced by trying to "play God," thinking that God should surrender to you, not you to Him.

Finally, think of what you are now, and what you could become with God. Don't live below your fullest potential as a Christian!

Q: What suggestions can you give to me when I have stopped questioning the will of God, but am having a hard time accepting it for what it is?—*S. M.*

A: First of all, it is encouraging to know that you have stopped questioning God's will! This is certainly a step in the right direction. When man places his limited knowledge and wisdom against the omniscient, all-knowing, infinite knowledge of God, he is "playing God" himself. This placing of self above God results in disillusionment and ultimate rejection by God (Matthew 7:21-23). It is unfortunate, however, that you are "having a hard time accepting it for what it is." That is, God's will is really an unpleasant revelation to you and meets resistance on your part. Apparently you are able to accept God's will intellectually but not emotionally.

May I suggest, S. M., that you first try to find out where the emotional resistance is coming from in your life. Perhaps you have already made up your mind what you want to do, and your displeasure or negative feeling in doing His will is because it is in conflict with your own. It may be that the problem is rooted in your lack of complete surrender to God and un-willingness to crucify (completely subdue) your own desires. Have you gone as far as the Garden of Gethsemane, but then backed off and failed to go on to the Cross?

On the other hand, it is quite possible that you have hidden resentments against God for imposing His will upon yours and thus restricting your freedom. Young people today are constantly emphasizing that they want to "do their own thing." They fail to realize that in insisting they be independent from God and others, they become slaves to their own selfishness. In reality, could it be you actually believe that real freedom is found in self-will rather than doing the will of God?

Finally, your difficulty in accepting God's will may be due to the sheer agony of facing suffering and hard-ship at times. Jesus, in His humanity, did not want to go to the Cross because of the normal tendency to escape pain and suffering. "Yet," He prayed, "not as I will, but as you will" (Matthew 26:39). A Christian puts his commitment first and his feelings last. Once your commitment and faith in God is firm, it is easier to accept His will "for what it is." In stepping out to do His will, regardless of the cost, you will then begin to un-derstand how His will is the very best possible way for you.

Q: My favorite Bible verse that I have kept my faith and belief in for quite a while is Romans 8:28. Does this verse hold true to me as a young person in the hard times I'm experiencing now?—*D. R.*

A: Please be assured, "that in all things God works for the good of those who love him, who have been called according to his purpose" (Romans 8:28). Don't let your faith waver in God's promise even in hard times!

Nevertheless, there is the danger of quoting the first part of this verse and failing to properly consider the second part. That is, some people tend to say, "in all things God works for the good," but they do not finish the verse, which includes the conditions of loving God and doing His will.

When a person does not finish the promise, this is called "sweet lemon" rationalization. This type of false reasoning and belief creates an overly optimistic type of Pollyanna world that does not consider the aspects of motivation, obedience, and responsibility.

You must be sure that you are loving God. Sometimes people try to use God for their own ends, coerce God into doing things for them or even ignore God rather than love Him, but still expect Him to work out everything for good. Also, there are some who love the world, their family, or themselves more than God and cling to the hope that everything will work out for the best.

The Bible says, "Do not love the world or anything in the world. If anyone loves the world, the love of the Father is not in him" (1 John 2:15). Jesus said, "Anyone who loves his father or mother more than me is not worthy of me; anyone who loves his son or daughter more than me is not worthy of me" (Matthew 10:37).

In order that all things work for good, you must do God's will. Ask yourself, D. R., if you are fitting into God's plans for your life. Disobedience, indifference, or carelessness can frustrate God's best for you.

The apostle Paul constantly did God's will in his many missionary journeys even though it took him through stripes, shipwrecks, and imprisonments. However, all that happened to him worked out for good. Think of how God used his life and gave us divinely revealed truth through Paul's letters included in our New Testament.

As you are experiencing hard times now, my friend, determine to love God and do His will; then rest in the faith that "in all things" God is working for your good!

Q: When the Holy Spirit is leading us, does He give us alternatives or more than one choice in situations?—*E. L.*

A: Your question, E. L., is particularly helpful because there are many good people who miss God's will in certain aspects of their lives and feel their whole lives are ruined because of this. This idea is due to their feeling that God is arbitrary, inflexible, and does not allow for alternatives.

Actually, insofar as His ideal will for anyone's life is concerned, God does not vacillate. That is, God is omniscient or all-wise, and He knows what is best for each individual. In this respect, He does not deliberately pick two or more plans for your life and then hope you will choose one of them. God's wisdom and love dictate that His first plan is always best.

Sometimes, of course, with your limited understanding of the future, you may find yourself questioning exactly what God's will is. The apostle Paul had fully intended to go into Asia, but God gave him a vision at night which indicated that he should go to Macedonia. To Paul, this new leading of God may have looked like an alternative, although it really was a part of God's established plan. Fortunately, after Paul had seen the vision, Luke records, "We got ready at once to leave for Macedonia" (Acts 16:10).

Thank God for sensitive Christians who walk in the

Spirit so carefully that God's leading can be detected each step of the way. God does have an ideal will for you every moment of your life if you seek to find it. Yet in His mercy and grace He allows for the effects of mistakes, sins, and disobedience which may—though need not—happen in your life. David certainly missed God's ideal will for his life because of his adulterous involvement with Bathsheba. But because he repented of this sin (Psalm 51), his life was not irreparably ruined; rather he again lived within the will of God, although it may have been according to an alternative plan.

When the Holy Spirit is leading you, His first choice is always best in all situations. However, if you fail in fulfilling that choice, God still has a plan for your life at every step if you will confess your self-will and be obedient to His new alternative.

HUMAN NATURE

Q: How can I learn not to be so selfish and self-centered?—*C. B.*

A: Selfishness, C. B., is misdirected love. It is love centered on the self instead of being directed out to God and others. It is love going in instead of out, and thus making the individual himself the end of his own affection. Like water going into a pool or lake without an outlet, it produces stagnation of pride, conceit, and superficial personal attachments.

The direction of one's love is determined by both innate and learned conditions. When the Bible states that we are sinners from birth, sinful from the time we were conceived (Psalm 51:5), this refers to the original sin or selfishness of all men. It is an innate, unlearned condition that is also called the "sinful mind" (Romans 8:7) and was brought about by the Fall.

One need not be a theologian or psychologist to be convinced of this innate selfishness. The loveliest child is selfish at birth and needs to be taught to be considerate of others. All children are ego-centered or self-centered. In fact, one of the main signs of maturity is the turning outward of love to others.

Nevertheless, as your question suggests, a person can become less selfish through learning. It is possible to partly change the direction of one's love. Some people become more loving through *associating with loving people.* They actually learn a new life-style through imitation. The good example of others has much to do with changing behavior.

On the other hand, some people learn to love when they become *involved in doing things for others.* The more they do for others, the greater their inner satisfaction or fulfillment. Man was made in the image of God, and God is love. The more he loves, the more he becomes like God, and this is the most fulfilling experience in life.

Some people learn to love more when they see *the negative consequences of selfishness.* When they see all the punishing effects of self-centeredness, it causes them to look for the rewards of love.

Of course, C. B., although natural efforts to love are important, perfect love can only be brought about by the supernatural power of the Holy Spirit. Only God can change innate selfishness into love!

Q: How does one obtain a sense of peace within oneself?—*L. G.*

A: The years of youth are times of unrest and conflict, and your search for peace within yourself is not easy. However, you can find peace, and I appreciate your letting me help you.

First of all, you can find peace within yourself through *self-understanding.* You have perhaps heard that "ignorance is bliss." Believe me, L. G., this is not true! People who ignore their conflicts, fears, and failures soon find themselves living a confused and unrealistic life. Theirs is the bliss of fantasy and phoniness. They are like the blind leading the blind. Peace within involves knowing your real self.

However, peace through self-understanding must be followed by *self-acceptance.* It is one thing to understand your inner characteristics, motives, and conflicts intellectually, but quite a different thing to accept yourself emotionally and be willing to change. Often people resent, deny, and defend themselves rather than face the truth. Theirs is the false peace of detachment from reality, and it ends in deep-seated unrest.

Next, peace within yourself comes from a sense of *self-fulfillment.* Modern psychology is emphasizing more and more the importance of living up to your fullest potential. It is not enough to merely maintain your existence and survival, but to go beyond survival to creativity and self-giving. The Bible makes it clear that we are made in God's image, and part of our destiny and sense of peace comes from the unfolding of our inner creative nature.

Finally, peace within oneself comes from *self-surrender.* It is at this point that a Christian finds the most complete peace possible. It is called in the Scriptures "the peace of God." The Bible says, "The peace of God, which transcends all understanding, will guard your hearts and your minds in Christ Jesus" (Philippians 4:7).

Surrender to God's law and will through faith in Christ brings peace from the guilt of sin and the bondage of selfishness. The Holy Spirit brings the fruit of peace in the inner self (Galatians 5:22).

Q: **Why can't I be satisfied with what I have?**—*Anonymous*

A: You may not be satisfied with what you have because you are unable to distinguish between your wants and your needs. We are living in a society where we are sold on the idea that if we do not have all the luxuries and push-button conveniences around us, we cannot be happy. The materialistic age in which we live emphasizes the importance of things at the expense of inner conditions of the mind and spirit.

Much of this preoccupation with externals and luxuries is due to the kind of high-pressure advertising we are subjected to through TV and other media. The psychology of advertising is to make people feel dissatisfied with what they have and sell them on new products, services, and experiences. By making all the "extras" of life seem indispensable to happiness, advertising keeps people dissatisfied with what they have, even though what they have may be entirely adequate for wholesome living.

The most satisfied people in life are those who can live on the level of need rather than wants and desires. You are probably not satisfied with what you have because you are living in a world of wish-fulfillment rather than a world of need-fulfillment. The Bible says to Christians that "God will meet all your needs according to his glorious riches in Christ Jesus" (Philippians 4:19). Notice that God does not promise to supply all your wants, but rather your *needs*.

Many people are not satisfied with what they have because they are not thankful. The Bible says, "Give thanks in all circumstances, for this is God's will for you in Christ Jesus" (1 Thessalonians 5:18). It also says, "And we know that in all things God works for the good of those who love him, who have been called according to his purpose" (Romans 8:28). Unthankful people are unhappy and dissatisfied people. They take for granted all the positive blessings they have. The fact that they can see and hear, have intelligence and sanity to adjust to life, and have good health means very little to them.

Fortunately, you can learn to be satisfied with what you have. Even the apostle Paul declared, "I have learned to be content whatever the circumstances" (Philippians 4:11). Learn to strip your life of the unnecessary wants, to be thankful for what you have, and above all to find God and His will for your life. Real satisfaction comes from within and does not need to be sustained by constant pleasures from without!

Q: What can be done about gossip?

A : Recently a teenager asked the question, "I'm in a youth group where the teenage Christian life is dying because of gossip. What can we do?"

Gossip, by definition, is idle talk about the affairs of others, and often leads to rumor and scandal, which is general talk that is damaging to a person's reputation. It is a serious problem which the apostle Peter listed with other major sins when he wrote, "If you suffer, it should not be as a murderer or thief or any other kind of criminal, or even as a meddler" (1 Peter 4:15).

James pointed up the terrible effects of gossip when he penned, "Likewise the tongue is a small part of the body, but it makes great boasts. Consider what a great forest is set on fire by a small spark. The tongue also is a fire . . . It corrupts the whole person, sets the whole course of his life on fire, and is itself set on fire by hell" (James 3:5-6).

People enjoy gossiping for different reasons, and none of them are motivated by love. Sometimes it is because a person is on an "ego trip" when he can be the first to tell something about somebody, whether it is true or not. It is like he is boasting, "Look who I am because of what I know!" Often gossip is a way of getting enjoyment out of the so-called misfortunes of others. The Bible says, "Love does not delight in evil but rejoices with the truth" (1 Corinthians 13:6). A person with a choice morsel of gossip frequently has almost a gleam in his eye as he tells it. He is often covering up his own sins and weaknesses by projecting them into others and hurting them.

What can be done about gossip? If you are aware of gossip, may I suggest that you do everything you can either privately or publicly to bring out the truth. However, do this with a humble, forgiving, and loving spirit. Let God's Holy Spirit work with you and through you to make things right. Be an example in your conversation (1 Timothy 2:8; James 3:2). By all means, "Love your neighbor as yourself" (Mark 12:33).

Q: A Christian is to be humble, but what about the need in many professions to promote yourself to survive in that area?—*C. B.*

A: Your question, C. B., points up a common conflict that many Christians have in trying to be successful without being self-assertive. It is easy to mistake humility for inferiority, meekness for weakness, or self-fulfillment for self-glory. However, the Bible clarifies these conflicts and leaves achievement possible. Humility is an attitude of heart toward what you are doing, but does not preempt your desire to do your best. True humility is actually a proper perspective of one's self.

For example, the apostle Paul wrote to his young friend Timothy, "If anyone sets his heart on being an overseer, he desires a noble task" (1 Timothy 3:1). He then goes on to emphasize the qualities and character of a good bishop rather than discourage a Christian from becoming one. Notice, too, that being a bishop was the highest office possible in the Church.

You see, the problem is not whether you should limit your goals, but what should be your ultimate purpose and motivation in reaching them. If a person desires the office of a bishop merely to inflate his own ego and promote himself, this is sinful. However, if he sees this attainment as providing a broader and more effective means of service to God and man, his motivation becomes righteous and holy.

When Jesus gave the parable of the talents in Matthew 25, He made it very clear that each person should use to the fullest the ability God has given him. In fact, the person who failed to use the one talent that he had, lost it, and he was called a "lazy servant."

Remember, C. B., nothing but your best pleases God the most!

Q: How can you love yourself without being egotistical?—*C. S.*

A: Self-acceptance is not self-centeredness, C. S.; egotistical people develop self-indulgent love for themselves to gain attention and enhance their importance and reputation. They become the end of their life, rather than a means to the end of loving God and others. They become vain, artificial, conceited, and have a flattering opinion of themselves. There is an absence of genuine humility and modesty; often in clever and subtle ways, they exalt themselves.

You can love yourself, C. S., without being egotistical. Start by having a *healthy sense of your own self-worth.* You were made in God's image and have an eternal soul. If for nothing else, love yourself for who you are and what you are in God's sight. You should not hate God's creation in you.

To love yourself without being egotistical is *Christian.* Jesus said, "Love your neighbor as yourself" (Matthew 22:39). The Bible encourages Christians to deny themselves, but not to hate themselves. Healthy self-love, important to Christian life, enables you to love others better. One who feels good about himself is more likely to feel good about others.

Also, *recognize the difference between sin and the sinner.* Many who hate and reject themselves fail to see this difference. God hates sin but loves the sinner.

"But because of his great love for us, God, who is rich in mercy, made us alive with Christ even when we were dead in transgressions—it is by grace you have been saved" (Ephesians 2:4-5). Don't hate yourself along with your sin.

Finally, you can love yourself more fully when *living a holy life.* It is difficult to love yourself if you feel condemned by sin or unholy feelings, which produce self-depreciation. When you let the Holy Spirit take complete control of your life, your love for yourself will come from a holy life, and not be egotistical.

Q: **Sometimes when people know you are a Christian, they take advantage of you because they think you are supposed to be generous, trusting, and loving. Should a Christian defend himself?—*E. M.***

A: When Jesus sent His disciples out to minister to others, E. M., He told them, "I am sending you out like sheep among wolves. Therefore be as shrewd as snakes and as innocent as doves" (Matthew 10:16). Although He expected them to love their neighbors as themselves (Mark 12:33), He also expected them to be wise and use good common sense in dealing with people. To be "innocent as doves" and show a Christian spirit of charity, mercy, and trust does not mean to be naive. The dictionary defines naive people as being sometimes foolishly simple, not suspicious; credulous (tending to believe too readily); and sometimes having an almost foolish lack of worldly wisdom.

But, there is a wisdom the world does not know. The Bible says, "Wisdom is better than folly, just as light is better than darkness" (Ecclesiastes 2:13). James described it, "Wisdom that comes from heaven is first of all pure; then peace loving, considerate, submissive, full of mercy and good fruit, impartial and sincere"

39

(3:17). Jesus demonstrated all these qualities James mentioned.

We may think of Jesus as meek and mild, but forget that this does not mean wishy-washy. He was strong and sensible. And He told His disciples to be strong and sensible. True, a Christian must be ready to witness to others at all times, but there is a time when, if the Word of God is despised and rejected, he must not be so gullible as to take unnecessary abuse and ridicule (Matthew 10:13, 14).

There were times, however, when Jesus allowed people to take advantage of Him. When it was His Father's will for Him to go to the Cross He suffered injustices and never opened His mouth in defense. God, in His wisdom, was working out His redemptive plan. Is the servant above his master? No. Contemporary Christians will also suffer some abuse, but sometimes the best defense is no defense at all.

THE LOCAL CHURCH

Q: **Can you be saved and not go to church? If so, would your relationship with God differ from someone who was saved through the church?—*J. C.***

A: We are living in a time when many people are rejecting the established, organized churches or denominations for various reasons. Some feel that the church has lost its evangelistic outreach, has deteriorated into nothing but a modified social "club," is too deeply concerned about arguing over theology, and does not appeal to the masses of people who want and need a personal relationship with Jesus Christ. Please be assured, J. C., that it is certainly possible to be saved outside the organized church, and that there are many churches that are spiritually dead. Nevertheless, the Bible is very clear in teaching that Christians should not abandon the fellowship of believers. In fact, many of the apostle Paul's Epistles in the Bible were written to churches.

To the Corinthians he wrote, "To the church of God in Corinth" (1 Corinthians 1:2). In greeting the Galatians he wrote, "To the churches in Galatia" (Galatians 1:2). His Epistles to the Thessalonians carry the salutation "To the church of the Thessalonians" (1 and 2 Thessalonians 1:1).

The Word of God reads, "Let us consider how we may spur one another on toward love and good deeds.

Let us not give up meeting together" (Hebrews 10:24-25).

In answer to your second question, J. C., a person's relationship with God would not differ whether he was saved through the organized church or out of it. However, the continuation of this relationship would certainly deteriorate if a Christian ignored the fellowship of believers. Don't ever underestimate the importance of fellowship in the life of Christians. In the Early Church, even though the Christians had to get together in the catacombs and risk their lives, they did not hesitate to do so. A united church is a stronger church. On the Day of Pentecost 120 believers were *united together* in spirit *in one place,* and the Holy Spirit came upon them.

Don't make the mistake of staying away from church. Your tithes, the love you demonstrate to others, and your united faith and witness enhance your relationship to God and man. In addition, we all need the encouragement and support that are available only within a loving, Spirit-filled body of believers.

Q: **Does the Bible condemn Christians who don't stick to one church but go to many churches?**—*S. W.*

A: To my knowledge, S. W., there is no specific scripture that condemns people for going to many different churches. However, there are certain biblical and psychological principles that make it advisable to maintain regular attendance at the same church.

The Bible warns against being influenced by every wind of doctrine, and thus becoming unstable in your beliefs (Ephesians 4:14). There is a danger of becoming involved in minor differences and making these a major part of your life and witness (Matthew 23:23). The apostle Paul warned Timothy, "Don't have anything to do with foolish and stupid arguments, because you know they produce quarrels" (2 Timothy 2:23).

Also, there is the tendency to attend the church that best fits your comfortable conscience than one which teaches truths which may disturb you and help you to grow spiritually. The Scripture says, "For the time will come when men will not put up with sound doctrine. Instead, to suit their own desires, they will gather around them a great number of teachers to say what their itching ears want to hear. They will turn their ears away from the truth and turn aside to myths" (2 Timothy 4:3-4).

Beware of becoming a "spiritual tramp" and thus avoiding the challenges that are a part of settling in one church. Many people who wander from one church to another are practicing escapism. That is, they stay in one church just long enough to avoid being involved in the hard work of leadership and loyalty. They are unpredictable and undependable, and really don't do any church permanent good.

Of course, there are always people who go from church to church in a never-ending "ego trip." Perhaps they have some special talent or are given special attention because they are newcomers. They stay in that church long enough for the glamor of their presence to wear off, and then move on.

One of the biggest problems of going from church to church is that a person's roots never go deep enough to produce a healthy spiritual life. As a consequence, their influence is very shallow and transient. Every church needs Christians who are "pillars" and help build "foundations" that keep the body of believers secure and steady.

Q: I have been to the altar and accepted Christ, but sometimes I still get bored in church. What advice can you give me?— *V. K.*

A: It is important for you to keep in mind, V. K., that when you become a Christian, you do not lose your humanity. Although you have established a spiritual relationship with God, you still are a physical, mental, and emotional being. You still have preferences or likes and dislikes, and you must continue to adjust to your environment. Your new relationship with God does not necessarily mean that all your contacts with people and institutions will be stimulating. For example, if a preacher continually talks in a droning monotone, uses big words or obscure theological terms, and speaks on subjects that are unrelated to your young life, it is often difficult not to get bored. Young people like to be challenged, to listen to sermons relative to their lives, and to be involved as much as possible in what is going on in the church.

Of course, the problem is not always with the preacher but with the institution of the church itself. Too much formality in the services, long drawn-out rituals, and little variety become tiresome. On the other hand, some services are so unstructured and unplanned that they become confusing. This, too, becomes boring if it occurs time after time.

Sometimes the problem of boredom lies within the person himself. If, for example, an individual is extremely tired or not feeling well physically, it is difficult to get interested in anything, including church services. Also, some people are constantly inattentive by habit, and others go to church so preoccupied with their own personal or emotional problems that they fail to focus on God and are not able to place these concerns in God's hands.

My advice to you is to consider the above factors as they relate to your boredom and to examine your real motivation for going to church in the first place. When a person becomes a Christian, his main concern should be to love, worship, praise, and serve God both in and out of church. Although the human factors enter in, you should constantly strive to keep your mind on Christ.

This means that when you find yourself getting bored

in church, you must often have to put aside the distracting and nonstimulating aspects of your environment, and worship God in spite of what is happening around you rather than because of it. Just as a musician transcends his world in song, and an artist in his painting, you must learn to reach out to God and worship Him despite an uninteresting, dull, and monotonous church service.

Q: How can a person be Christian without being phony?—*J. W.*

A: Keep in mind, J. W., that some non-Christians will call you phony no matter what you do. It is their subtle and defensive way of denying God's claims upon their lives through belittling any witness.

Nevertheless, there are certain characteristics that turn off non-Christians and create genuine doubts about the nature of a true follower of Christ. Perhaps the following observations will help you.

Non-Christians can accept both you and your faith more readily when you act like yourself in your witness. Be yourself! That is, refrain from using the stereotyped words and phrases of others, and try not to force a testimony that makes the situation awkward and tense. Timing is very important, and you tend to appear more like your real self when you are relaxed and comfortable in your witness.

Learn to say no in a gracious but firm manner. Christians who compromise their convictions for the sake of conformity, popularity, and acceptance are phony.

Make your Christian life attractive to non-Christians. Too many times nonbelievers reject so-called Christians because they seem to say one thing and live another. That is, they talk about happiness, peace, or love, but appear to be unhappy, distressed, and critical or bitter. There is something contagious about a true Christian life with "abundant living."

Finally, look upon non-Christians not only as eternal souls, but people as well. There are some phony Christians who seem to love souls but hate and reject people.

Jesus not only loved the souls of men, but He really cared about them as persons. He healed them and loved them. Don't be a Pharisee and become exclusive, self-righteous, and prejudiced. Let love for all be the trademark of your Christian witness.

Q: When a person who is a Christian at camp goes back home and becomes just a regular around non-Christians, do you think he is really a Christian or simply putting on an act?—*B. V.*

A: It usually is easier, B. V., to live a Christian life around other Christians than when one is among people who do not know Christ. The apostle Peter found this to be true when he denied three times in a row that he knew Jesus. As a result he felt discouraged and condemned.

There is a difference, however, between a hypocrite and a Christian who in his weakness yields to temptation. A hypocrite is a person who knows he is not a Christian, but deliberately fakes people out by putting on religious acts. Jesus issued severe warnings to such persons.

On the other hand, there is the Christian who sincerely wants to live a Christian life but yields to temptation during times of weakness. Peter was not a hypocrite; nevertheless, he *did* deny Christ, sinning against Him when tempted in moments of weakness.

A genuine Christian does not want to sin. Fortunately, there are some things he can do to keep from sinning and to overcome his weakness. Peter was later filled with the Holy Spirit and became strong in the Lord. Sin occurs when we give in to the weakness of our humanity. However, the Bible says, "Live by the Spirit, and you will not gratify the desires of the sinful nature" (Galatians 5:16).

Seek to be filled with the Holy Spirit, and also build up your faith through prayer and reading your Bible. Remember, Scripture says, "My grace is sufficient for you, for my power is made perfect in weakness" (2 Corinthians 12:9). God can make you more than "just regular" around non-Christians!

Q: Can a psychiatrist be of help to a Christian? Why do some Christians feel that psychotherapy undermines a Christian's faith?—*P. B.*

A: Perhaps the main reason why some Christians hesitate to seek help from a psychiatrist is because they fail to see the relationship between the natural and the supernatural worlds. That is, they make the mistake of interpreting all problems as spiritual, and thus they reject any help that is not considered divine.

Also, some Christians erroneously envision all sickness as directly related to sin. In fact, the disciples made this mistake. When they saw the blind man, they asked, "'Rabbi, who sinned, this man or his parents, that he was born blind?'

"'Neither this man nor his parents sinned,' said Jesus, 'but this happened so that the work of God might be displayed in his life'" (John 9:2-3).

In addition, there are some Christians who, although they will go to a medical doctor who is not a psychiatrist and accept physical illness as something that can be cured with natural treatment, do not consider that emotional problems can have other than spiritual causes. Thus, they reject any psychotherapy or mental health procedures.

Under certain conditions a psychiatrist can be of help to a Christian. For example, not all depression is caused by spiritual problems. I know of a young lady whose overactive thyroid gland prevented her from sleeping properly. After weeks of sleep loss she became very depressed. When the thyroid condition was corrected, she brightened up and her deep depression disappeared. A psychiatrist is also a medical doctor and can help with these distinctions.

Psychiatry does not need to undermine a Christian's faith if he fully understands that man is affected by both natural and supernatural laws of the universe. It is not a breach of faith in God to cure emotional or physical illness using natural therapy.

Nevertheless, P. B., I hesitate, to refer Christians, or anyone, to psychiatrists who are not Christians themselves. Too often they try to play God and minimize, if not ridicule, spiritual causes. While some Christians believe that all emotional or physical problems have only spiritual causes, some psychiatrists take the opposite extreme and believe all problems have only natural causes. Both are wrong!

It takes a Christian psychiatrist usually to understand the relationships between the natural and supernatural worlds. Often non-Christian psychiatrists can do more harm than good when they fail to consider the spiritual perspective.

Q: Should a Christian feel defeated or a failure if he or she seeks professional help from a psychologist?—*S. L.*

A: Your question points up the fairly typical conflict Christians have in questioning their faith and experience when considering psychological problems. They do not hesitate to seek medical help with a physical problem, but hesitate to apply natural laws and principles to mental and emotional problems.

Part of this dilemma stems from a failure to distinguish between psychological and spiritual problems, and between the natural and supernatural. For example, it is natural to have moods, as in the situation when "Jesus wept" (John 11:35). It is natural to want friends and to escape loneliness. Jesus loved to visit in the home of Martha, Mary, and Lazarus.

To be spiritual is not to be less than human. The apostle Paul says, "We have this treasure in jars of clay" (2 Corinthians 4:7). No one can escape the interaction between the physical and the spiritual, the secular and the sacred.

Personality problems are frequently related to spiritual problems, but many times they are not. People, because of their backgrounds, learn the wrong ways to think, to feel, and to act in life situations. They experience many conflicts and emotional reactions that reflect frustrations caused by habits, attitudes, and perceptions not necessarily related to their spiritual lives.

Nevertheless, if you should seek psychological help, you would be wise to find a Christian psychologist, Secular psychology is so preoccupied with the social and physical environments of people and things that it ignores the spiritual world.

Also, a Christian psychologist is more likely to have a healthier balance between what is learned and what is innate. For example, all the natural learning that can be applied will not change or remove sin from one's life. Only God can change some aspects of our personality and replace selfishness with love.

Using professional help is not a breach of faith, but it can be God's way of helping you solve your problem.

SANCTIFICATION

Q: It is harder to live the sanctified life than just being saved. Since I can go to heaven by being only saved, why be sanctified or filled with the Holy Spirit?—*C. B.*

A: Your question is a good one, C. B., and reveals the thinking of many other teenagers and adults, as well. It is indeed harder to live the Spirit-filled life, and many people feel comfortable settling for less.

You are correct in your statement that a person can be saved or born again and go to heaven without experiencing the sanctified life. The apostle Paul wrote the Corinthian church, "Brothers, I could not address you as spiritual but as worldly—mere infants in Christ. I gave you milk, not solid food, for you were not yet ready for it. Indeed, you are still not ready. You are still worldly" (1 Corinthians 3:1-3).

The Corinthians were born again, because Paul called them "infants in Christ." However, he does not condone many of the attitudes they were displaying. In fact, he spends most of the remainder of his letter to the Corinthians in pointing out their need for a deeper work of grace which ultimately centers in love (13:1-13).

Please be assured, however, that when Paul, through divine revelation, gave the Corinthian believers new light about living the Christian life, they could no longer settle for their old ways. This is because that once the truth about entire sanctification is made known to a Christian, he becomes disobedient to God if he does not respond to this light by seeking after the blessing of holiness. At this point his salvation is brought into jeopardy. The Bible does not encourage or reward disobedience. Thus the Christian cannot settle for less than what he knows God wants him to experience.

God's Word says, "But if we walk in the light, as he is in the light, we have fellowship with one another, and the blood of Jesus, his Son, purifies us from every sin" (1 John 1:7). "Anyone, then, who knows the good he ought to do and doesn't do it, sins" (James 4:17). Nowhere in the Bible is it taught that there will be sin in heaven—and disobedience is sin.

Finally, Jesus warned, "Not everyone who says to me, 'Lord, Lord,' will enter the kingdom of heaven, but only he who does the will of my Father who is in heaven" (Matthew 7:21). It is God's will for Christians to be wholly sanctified or filled with the Spirit (1 Thessalonians 5:23; Hebrews 13:12). Don't lose your salvation by ignoring the Holy Spirit's call to holiness (1 Thessalonians 4:7), but actively seek to be made holy, as "it is God's will that you should be holy" (v. 3).

Q: **Is sanctification a growing experience or does it just happen?**—*Anonymous*

A: Sanctification—or to be more precise, *entire sanctification*—is a second work of grace which follows a Christian's initial experience of salvation or that of being born again. It is not gradual, but happens at a given point in time. This is true for at least two reasons.

First, God is a *person;* and when an individual is filled with the Holy Spirit, or entirely sanctified, there is an immediate awareness of that Person—the Spirit of God. By definition, entire sanctification is to be cleansed wholly from your sin and filled with the Holy

Spirit; and this is not the gradual oozing of some power or atmosphere into man's personality and soul.

There are numerous instances in the Bible where this immediate relationship between God and man is demonstrated. However, the baptism or infilling of the Holy Spirit at Pentecost best illustrates the fact that entire sanctification is not gradual. There were 120 Christians in the Upper Room praying and waiting for the fulfillment of Christ's promise to send the Holy Spirit (Acts 1:5). The Holy Spirit came upon them all at the same time, and this was not gradual.

Second, to be wholly sanctified, a Christian must consecrate his whole life to God without reservation. He must *will* to allow God to become not only his Savior from sin, but complete Lord and sovereign authority in his life. Events and experiences that lead up to this commitment may be gradual, but the ultimate decision of the will happens at a given point in time.

Many Christians confuse entire sanctification with growth in grace. You cannot *grow into* entire sanctification because this is a gift of God. The Holy Spirit is given, as at Pentecost, when consecration and faith are complete, and when God chooses to bestow His Spirit. On the other hand, a sanctified Christian can *grow in* the relationship. He can grow in his capacity to experience God, to discern His will, to understand His Word, to express His love, and in many other ways. Also, there are many traits, attitudes, likes, dislikes, and other personality characteristics that are learned which can be changed to make a person a better Christian.

The apostle Paul, although he was filled with the Spirit, said, "I have *learned* to be content whatever the circumstances" (Philippians 4:11). He learned patience and thus grew in grace in his sanctified experience. It takes both entire sanctification and growth in grace to be a mature Christian.

Q: In the Bible it says we should follow holiness, and without it "no one will see the Lord." Is holiness or sanctification a requirement for admission into heaven?— *H. L.*

A: The Bible teaches that man can not only be forgiven for the acts of sin and be born again, but he can also be filled with the Holy Spirit and be perfectly pure and holy in heart (Acts 15:8-9).

However, the scripture you have quoted does not necessarily refer to the doctrine of holiness as such. It does not mean that everyone who is not entirely sanctified will not go to heaven and see God. There is no evidence in the Word of God (Luke 23:40-43) that the penitent thief on the cross had reached the state of being perfectly holy. He did confess to Christ that he was a sinner and asked His help. Jesus then said unto him, "I tell you the truth, today you will be with me in paradise" (v. 43).

One of the best explanations of the verse "Without holiness no one will see the Lord" (Hebrews 12:14) is found in *Transformed Christians,* a book by Col. Milton S. Agnew of The Salvation Army. On page 164 he points out that the word "see" is the Greek word *horao,* which often depicts *discernment* more than sight.

In fact, he notes, it is the same Greek word Jesus used when He said, "Blessed are the pure in heart, for they will see God" (Matthew 5:8). It's the "see" the blind man uses when he comprehends something and exclaims, "Oh, now I see!" What this verse is saying, H. L., is that God is holy, and without some degree of holiness man cannot understand, detect, or identify the true nature and person of God. He cannot correctly perceive or discern what God is like.

The critical issue as to the degree of holiness necessary for the admission of a Christian into heaven centers around whether a person is walking or living in all the light or knowledge he has been given. The Bible makes a distinction between "infants in Christ" and mature Christians (1 Corinthians 3:1; 13:1-13). However, failure to obey God's will at any stage in a person's life disqualifies him or her for admission to heaven (Matthew 7:21-23).

 Once Christians are saved and sanctified, why do we still sin?—*J. K.*

A: Being free from sin and Holy Spirit-filled is no guarantee that a person cannot sin again. God created man higher than animals, with a free will. Heredity, environment, and even the spiritual changes you mention do not supersede man's right to later choose against God's will and thus sin.

Adam and Eve, created in God's image, perfectly holy, still sinned. Jesus was perfectly holy too, and yet in His humanity, not His divinity, He was tempted to sin. Temptation would be meaningless without something in Him that could respond. He could have chosen not to go the Cross, but He chose His Father's will (Matthew 26:39). He never sinned because He chose not to yield to the temptation.

The world, the flesh, and the devil are three major sources of temptation. Christians are not immune from these influences. Paul said, "Demas, because he loved this world, has deserted me" (2 Timothy 4:10). We are constantly tempted to love things, pleasures, and people, to lose our souls by putting other things before God (Matthew 10:37-38).

One powerful temptation is for man to trust the flesh and become self-sufficient. Paul asked, "Are you so foolish? After beginning with the Spirit, are you now trying to attain your goal by human effort?" (Galatians 3:3). Even after a person is saved and sanctified, he can direct his attention away from God and toward the works and desires of the flesh.

Finally, the Scriptures clearly reveal Satan as a reality. He tempted Adam and Eve, and Christ, and "prowls around like a roaring lion looking for someone to devour" (1 Peter 5:8).

Those saved and sanctified can sin. Neglect of prayer, Bible reading, and living by the Spirit weakens resistance to evil and makes it easier to choose wrongly and sin. But God's grace can keep man from falling if he will choose to do God's will.

SEX, DATING, MARRIAGE

Q: Taking into account the world's constant change, how can we be assured that the person we choose to marry will be able to meet our changing needs for the rest of our lives? Can we fall out of love?—*J. E., M. H., M. M.*

A: This is the first time I have received a question signed by three young people, and this adds to the seriousness of your concern. It is my hope that this answer will be of help to you. The answer to your question depends upon the kind of love you are talking about. As you may know, there are different kinds of love that motivate people to marry. Specifically, there are four.

Neurotic love is the feeling that "I love you because I need you." It is motivated by the need for personal security rather than a genuine attachment and concern for the other person. It is easy for people with neurotic love to "fall out of love" because they only love someone who constantly meets their needs. When their needs change their love disappears. This kind of love is basically selfish, and marriages based only on need satisfaction are on an extremely shaky foundation.

Erotic love is sexual attachment, and this kind of love is subject to constant changes throughout life. Certainly one would be unwise to marry if there were no erotic or romantic sexual love involved. On the other hand, it is inevitable that individual needs for sexual love will vary considerably in different people at different times and age levels. We are living in a changing world, as your question states. Unfortunately, changes are often in the wrong direction. Too much emphasis is being placed today upon the importance of sex, both in and out of marriage. As someone has said, "Isn't love gland!" Those who let their glands dictate their love life fall in and out of love strictly because of physiological changes, and their marriage status changes with their sexual needs and satisfactions only.

Transference love is loving someone because they are like somebody you have loved earlier in life, such as a parent. This kind of "love by association" is quite symbolic and does not stand the test of reality in marriage. A husband should not be his wife's father, and a wife is not a man's mother. This confusion in roles does not build stable marriages.

Real love is loving a person for what he or she is as a person, rather than what needs are met, sex is provided, or pleasant associations are recalled. It is love that gives rather than seeks to receive, that is willing to make a commitment "until death do us part," and that is motivated by inner dedication and faithfulness instead of the outer changes in the environment or world. People with real love work to grow in love through constant sacrifice, understanding, and acceptance.

Q: How long should you go with a girl you love before getting married?—*K. D.*

A: Although there is no standard length of time for engagements, K. D., the most sensible time to get married is when you have reasonably matured in all the major areas of your life. Chances of staying married increase, in general, with age. Statistically and actually your teenage years are not the best time to make a commitment for a lifetime.

The time that you go together depends upon various conditions in the life of both parties. For example, chronological age is only one of the factors involved. Social age is a very important aspect to consider in marriage. That is, young people who are too dependent upon their parents, are extremely withdrawn from people, and have difficulty adjusting to authority find marriage difficult.

Your moral and spiritual ages are important, too. A man or woman who vacillates on what is right in fidelity to his mate sexually is no candidate for marriage. To be spiritually mature enough to marry, you need to reach a place where you are willing to do God's will and be morally responsible.

An engagement should also be long enough for couples to reasonably understand each other. Although marriage is founded on love, it is enhanced and sustained by mutual understanding. Engaged couples should take enough time to learn about each other's interests, values, family background, attitudes toward family life, and spiritual beliefs and experience.

The degree to which couples understand each other is determined by how frequently they can be together, their openness in sharing, and the number and variety of experiences they have to learn about each other. Some individuals are inhibited, shy, and very reluctant to share their inner life. This type of person usually needs a longer engagement period than one who is outgoing, open, and candid.

Finally, give yourself adequate time to be sure that your attachment to your girl friend is based on real love and not infatuation. Real love is based upon what your girl is as a person, but infatuation is founded largely on sexual attachment alone. Go with your girl friend long enough to know that you really love her, to be sure you are doing God's will, and that you are mature enough to be a responsible husband.

Q: **Should we act like a Christian on a date if our boyfriend is not a Christian, because we want to make a good impression?—*C. K.***

A: First of all, C. K., a Christian ought to beware of dating non-Christians. There is no guarantee that your boyfriend (or girl friend) will ever turn to Christ. There are many, many Christian young people who are tempted to compromise their convictions for romance. The natural attraction to the opposite sex, the fear of rejection, and the ultimate desire to marry and have a family create special pressures during the teenage years.

The crux of your question, however, is really not whether you should become a phony Christian to make a good impression on your date. If you are a true Christian, you know deep down in your heart that Jesus Christ and what He stands for must always come first, regardless of the circumstances or people in your life. The Bible says, "You cannot drink the cup of the Lord and the cup of demons too; you cannot have a part in both the Lord's table and the table of demons" (1 Corinthians 10:21). "He is a double-minded man, unstable in all he does" (James 1:8). You must maintain your convictions and standards if you are to remain a Christian, whether in dating or anything else.

Nevertheless, C. K., your idea of what it means to "act like a Christian" may be somewhat distorted at times. That is, a Christian is not a bore. Rather, a Christian should have fun, be friendly, show a good disposition, and be a person with a pleasing personality. Unfortunately, young people are too frequently taught the negative aspects of religion, and often the models they are supposed to imitate give the wrong impression of a true follower of Christ. They are raised on a diet of "don'ts" and do not have a clear understanding of the "do's." The emphasis is too much on the negative and not enough on the positive in Christian living.

Believe me, C. K., if your boyfriend is any kind of

person with character and principles at all, even if he is not a Christian, he will be attracted to you, and Christ, more strongly if you come through as a girl who can have a good time without compromising your standards.

Q: There is a Christian girl whom I love very much and would like to marry. However, I'm not the Christian I should be and can't get back on track. What can I do? —*S. N.*

A: It is encouraging to know, S. N., that you realize your marriage would not be complete when your spiritual life is not right. However, it is discouraging to learn that you "can't get back on track." May I suggest possible reasons why you are not the Christian person you should be.

First, your statement "I can't" is probably better stated, "I won't get back on track." Often *willpower* is overwhelmed by "want" power, for people wind up doing what they really want to do first. The personality is made up of intellect, feeling, and will. The way a person thinks or feels profoundly affects his decisions of the will. He does not act with conviction, dedication, and determination if he continually gives in to his thoughts and emotions.

May I suggest that you read the classic book *The Christian's Secret of a Happy Life,* and particularly the chapter entitled "Difficulties Concerning the Will." The author, Hannah Whitall Smith, vacillated in her Christian experience but eventually found the secret of living a consistent spiritual life: "Now, the truth is, that this (Christian) life is not to be lived in the emotions at all, but in the will."

This was the secret of how our Lord Jesus Christ overcame temptation and went to the Cross. In the Garden of Gethsemane He was faced with a decision of His will that was extremely difficult to make. In His humanity He did not want to go to the Cross, but He did not give in to His feelings. He made a decision of His will to do His Father's will!

Second, your statement "I can't" is probably better stated, "I do not have *faith* enough to get back on track." That is, your faith may rest in your own righteousness, wisdom, or strength instead of the grace and power of God. The apostle Paul said, "I can do everything through him who gives me strength" (Philippians 4:13). Faith in Christ gives victory!

Finally, to say, "I can't," probably means, "I don't really want to make the *sacrifices* necessary to get back on track." The Christian life is not an easy life to live. Jesus said, "Broad is the road that leads to destruction, and many enter through it. But small is the gate and narrow the road that leads to life, and only a few find it" (Matthew 7:13-14). To "get back on track" and enter into a happy marriage to the girl you love, S. N., you may need to sacrifice such attachments as your love of the world, personal desires, or secret sins. Will you do it?

Q: **What words of advice can you give a person before they get married?—*S. M.***

A: In contemplating your question, S. M., two of the most important factors you should consider are whether the marriage is God's will for you and is motivated by genuine love. To leave God out of marriage assumes that a person's own wisdom is enough to make one of the major decisions of his or her life. In a sense, many people are "playing God" themselves by being so self-sufficient! You see, S. M., on the surface a godless marriage may have every appearance of being a successful one according to society's standards. However, according to God's eternal plan for the lives involved, it may be a miserable failure. A marriage that does not honor God, that produces a family who does not glorify Him and whose members do not become a part of the "family of God" as Christians, falls far short of God's eternal purpose and plan for both parents and children.

Before getting married, both parties should be absolutely sure that their love is genuine. Strangely enough, many people marry for reasons other than love. For example, some marry merely to satisfy their needs for security. Others marry out of loneliness and their need for acceptance and companionship. Still others give in to the pressures of persuasion from their families, to avoid some possible social stigma in being single, or to conform to the expectancies of their peers and friends. Some marry merely for the comfort and convenience of having a home. Real love is not based so much on whether your own personal needs are met, but on how you can meet the needs and enhance the happiness of your mate. It is not selfish, but self-sacrificing. Genuine love is not giving in to pressures from without, but is motivated by deep affection and devotion from within.

Emotional maturity is also important before marriage. Contrary to what many young people think, marriage does not solve all your problems. People who are unstable emotionally with serious depressions, fears, and eccentric symptoms are poor risks in marriage.

Finally, although the Bible does not demand that the parties involved have their parents' approval when they are of age, it is extremely important that this be worked out as graciously as possible. The three major causes of divorce today are money, sex, and in-laws (not necessarily in this order). Be sure you understand the sexual implications of marriage, and also do all you can to bring the parents of both families into an acceptance of your marriage plans.

Q: How important is sex in the life of a Christian?—*A. W.*

$A:$ Sex, my young friend, is as important in the life of a Christian as it is in the life of anyone else. Although a Christian should not be obsessed with sex like so many young people in this generation, neither can a Christian afford to deny, ignore, or minimize the strength, persistence, and importance of the sex drive.

A Christian should realize that, although the most precious part of his life is his salvation from sin and God's presence, the Bible says, "We have this treasure in jars of clay" (2 Corinthians 4:7). Sometimes Christian young people are taught that sexual feelings are bad and should be ignored. However, this is not the case. How can a person remain well adjusted and deny one of the most powerful biological drives in his life?

A Christian has normal and natural sex drives, and they are not to be taken lightly. However, important as it is to recognize and accept humanity, it is also important to learn how to control it. How a person adjusts to the sex drive can either make or break his moral, spiritual, social, and even physical life.

It is not unchristian to have thoughts about sex. The biology of sexual life alone, like hunger, pushes its way into the conscious minds of everyone. A Christian can no more deny that he feels sexual impulses than that he has hunger cravings. However, it is extremely important to control these thoughts and feelings and avoid lust. Lust is the desire to seek unrestrained gratification of sexual impulses by exploiting others through fornication (sexual intercourse between single men and women before marriage) and adultery (sexual intercourse by marrieds with someone other than their wife or husband).

Also, in courtship before marriage young people sometimes engage in such heavy petting that they overstimulate the sex drive and initiate unnecessary temptations. A Christian who accepts the importance of sex and learns to control and channel his sexual desire has a better chance to have a balanced sex life in marriage. Don't underestimate the importance of sex in the life of a Christian, A. W.; and strive, with God's help, to control and channel sexual impulses into holy and righteous living.

Q: How should we respond to fellow Christians who can accept abortion?—*L. M.*

A: In answer to your question, L. M., I wish I could say that it is merely a difference of opinion on abortion, and you should merely be tolerant of their belief and make no response. However, the problem of abortion has too many moral and spiritual implications to dismiss it so lightly.

In the first place, most of the problems of abortion are not produced because of danger to the mother or the possibility of the child being born deformed or impoverished mentally. Most abortions are a direct result of the sins of fornication and adultery. Anyone, Christian or not, who chooses to destroy human life merely to protect their pride or family name, or for their own convenience, is sinning against God and man, in addition to the poor unborn child who is deprived of life. Your response to fellow Christians, assuming that they are truly born again, is to ask them what made the abortion necessary. If a person accepts abortion under the conditions of fornication or adultery, he is not merely mistaken, but is placing himself in opposition to God and His laws.

Your Christian friends may be confused as to the difference between the penalty for sin and the consequences of sin. Christ died on the Cross to pay the penalty for sin when a person is willing to confess it, repent, and accept His forgiveness. However, Christ did not die to remove all the consequences of sin.

The truth of the matter is that people who have abortions due to illicit sex are trying to minimize the consequences of their lust by denying life to an unborn child. They want the innocent child to pay the consequences. How selfish can people get! Can they imagine Jesus telling others to cover up lust with death? Christians cannot condone and accept abortion under these circumstances. You should respond to your fellow Christians by helping them think through these implications of abortion, resulting in a more positive solution to the situation.

Nevertheless, if your friends accept abortion as a merciful act to save one life, there is more room for debate and difference of opinion. In this case, the motivation for having the child is not sponsored by sin, and the consequences are not selfish but humanitarian.

Q: **What kind of stand should a Christian take in regard to the "gay movement"?** —*J. B.*

A: Your question, J. B., refers to a movement and, consequently, approaches homosexual behavior from the standpoint of the whole group. People with homosexual problems, whether they be hidden tendencies or actual participation in homosexual acts, need our empathy, help, and fervent prayers. Many of them not only are struggling with the problem of personal guilt and torment, but social rejection as well. Jesus did not compromise with sin, but He did show compassion.

Nevertheless, a Christian should not support the gay movement for at least two reasons. First, there is little, if any, attempt on the part of many of those involved to change their behavior. You see, J. B., there are really two kinds of homosexuals. There are those who are making an honest attempt to find help and spiritual victory, and there are those who have become hardened in what they are doing and openly defy God and man to change them. Many of the latter category constitute the gay movement.

Second, a Christian should not support the gay

movement because group activity of this kind minimizes personal responsibility. That is, each person involved tends to identify with the group to such an extent that his own personal conscience is weakened, and he externalizes his guilt rather than internalizes it. He becomes associated with the collective conscience of the group and thus bypasses a certain sense of individual morality.

This happened to the apostle Paul before he committed his life to Christ, when he held the coats of those who stoned Stephen to death (Acts 7:57-60). He hid his own hatred and animosity behind the activities of the group and thus soothed his troubled conscience. When this is done, conscience and reality are replaced by conformity, and the blame is placed upon the group. A Christian should not support any movement that rids him of personal responsibility to God and man.

Q: What if you should care about Christ, but don't, and you really don't want to care?—*K. H.*

A: Fortunately, by admitting your true feelings in asking this question, K. H., you have already taken the first step in correcting your condition. You are not a phony or hypocrite, even though you know what you ought to do. We are told in the Scriptures to examine ourselves whether we be in the faith, and this you are doing.

The truth of the matter is that no one really cares about or loves Christ first. The Bible says, "We love because he first loved us" (1 John 4:19), and this God understands. The uniqueness of Christ is that He cares about us even when we do not care about Him. This is divine love.

Jesus said, "If you love those who love you, what reward will you get?" (Matthew 5:46). He loves the unlovable and the sinner.

Assuming your belief in Christ, not caring for Him and not really wanting to care is rooted in selfishness or self-love. However, in examining yourself you may find other reasons too. As a young person you are no doubt striving for independence and occasionally have trouble with authority. Since God is an authority figure, you may class Him with all other types of authority and reject Him for this reason.

Some young people don't want to care about Christ because it involves commitment and sacrifice. To really care about Him would mean that they would have to give up certain associations, pleasures, or plans.

You know you should care about Christ, and you have been honest enough to admit it. Face up to the true reason, and then ask God to forgive you for Jesus' sake. The gift of God's forgiveness and love will make you want to care about Christ.

Q: **Why do I feel so guilty when the job I'm applying for requires leadership qualities and I have none?—S. R.**

A: It seems to me that your question not only involves feelings of guilt but also inferiority! When you said, in regard to leadership qualities, that you have "none," this attitude could very well be the real problem. There are very few people, if any, who are completely void of leadership skills.

In fact, when you took the initiative to apply for a job or to ask this question, you displayed a leadership quality. One of the most important aspects of good leadership is being aggressive and taking the initiative. This you have done in the above two instances, and probably in many, many others.

Leadership also involves being friendly, industrious, conscientious, and having purpose. People who are leaders are cooperative, have desire, and strive to succeed. Can you honestly say that you have none of these characteristics?

Actually, recent surveys demonstrate that more people are successful in jobs due to their personality characteristics than either their technical skills or level of education. What you are as a person is ultimately more important in leadership than other qualities.

It is quite possible, S. R., that most of your guilt feelings stem from a perfectionist attitude. Perfectionists make the mistake of doing what is called "either-or thinking." That is, they see themselves as either a great success or a miserable failure. There is no middle ground in their thinking that allows for anything but "all-or-none" performance.

Usually the goals of perfectionists are too high, too vague, or too unrealistic. When the goals are too high, they can never reach them. If they are too vague, they never know when they have succeeded; and if they are too unrealistic, they are impossible to reach. As a result they blame themselves for their failures and feel guilty.

May I suggest that you take a long look at your self-concept. Be more realistic than idealistic in what you expect of yourself. Build on the qualities you have rather than give up because of the characteristics you may not possess. Develop a positive attitude toward yourself, and above all have faith in God and seek to do His will!

Q: There are times when I feel emotionally down, even as a Christian, and I just can't seem to have enough faith. Do you have any suggestions to help me?—*S. H.*

A: One of the most common conflicts in young Christians like you is to confuse feelings with faith. No individual anywhere, whether Christian or non-Christian, has an emotional life that is always the same. Changes in moods and feelings inevitably occur and may be due to either inner or outer conditions.

The Bible records that "Jesus wept" (John 11:35). He was emotionally down both at the death of Lazarus and when He looked over Jerusalem and realized how many people there had rejected His plan of salvation from sin (Luke 19:41-44). Jesus in His humanity experienced sadness because of His loss of a dear friend, the suffering of others in the family, and the knowledge that those who rejected Him would be eternally separated from God.

The apostle Paul recognized the human factors in Christian living when he wrote, "We have this treasure in jars of clay to show that this all-surpassing power is from God and not from us" (2 Corinthians 4:7). He suffered many physical and emotional setbacks but kept his faith strong. The secret to his victorious life was that he did not direct his faith toward either his feelings, his intellectual understanding of everything that happened, or circumstances around him. His faith rested in a personal relationship with Jesus Christ.

Your faith, S. H., will not thrive on fluctuating feelings but on your constant commitment to God. God is a person who knows, understands, and cares about you. He has the power, wisdom, and love to be worthy of your trust. The next time you get "emotionally down," don't lose your faith. Look up to God and keep your faith directed toward Him.

Q: How does the Holy Spirit help you handle such temptations as drinking and drugs?—*M. M.*

A: First of all, M. M., the Bible says, "Since we live by the Spirit, let us keep in step with the Spirit" (Galatians 5:25). There are many Christians who find the life of the Spirit, but fail to "keep in step with the Spirit" day by day. The Scriptures make it clear that there is always, even in the life of the most saintly, a constant battle with the flesh. The apostle Paul recognized this and said to the Galatian Christians, "Live by the Spirit, and you will not gratify the desires of the sinful nature" (v. 16). The Holy Spirit will help you handle temptations if you do not quench or resist His work in your life each day.

Nevertheless, it is a well-known fact that there are

deep and binding habits that grip people strictly through the process of learning. People learn from their environment, either through imitation of others, reinforcement of habit due to the momentary satisfaction and the tension reduction it brings, or because their conformity to such behavior as drinking and drugs gives them acceptance in a group they consider important. That is, they become psychologically addicted to habits which indirectly meet other needs in their lives.

To change learning there must be a change in motivation. That is, the inner desires of an individual must be changed before learning habits can be eliminated. The Holy Spirit helps people handle temptation and habits by putting within them a love for God, for others, and for themselves. This change in motivation becomes greater than their desire to sin. The Bible says, "The one who is in you is greater than the one who is in the world" (1 John 4:4). The Holy Spirit alters motivation so that new and positive learning can take place.

Finally, one of the greatest attributes of the Spirit is His supernatural power. The Scripture says, "You will receive power when the Holy Spirit comes on you" (Acts 1:8). Power means "the ability to do, act, or produce in various situations of life." Power means to have vigor, force, and strength as opposed to weakness. The power of the Holy Spirit not only strengthens human capacities but nullifies the power of Satan as well. The energy and ability that the Holy Spirit brings will enable you to say, along with the apostle Paul, "I can do everything [including resisting alcohol and drugs] through him who gives me strength" (Philippians 4:13).

Q: **Is it possible for a Christian to fall away from Christ?**—*F. H.*

A: Backsliding, or the "falling away of the soul from God after having been saved," is a definite possibility as taught in the Scriptures. There are many references in the Bible to having known and followed Christ and then falling away from Him. For example, when Jesus taught about the relationship of the branches (Christians) to the Vine (Christ). He said, "If anyone does not remain in me, he is like a branch that is thrown away and withers; such branches are picked up, thrown into the fire and burned" (John 15:6). Jesus also said, "No one who puts his hand to the plow and looks back is fit for service in the kingdom of God" (Luke 9:62).

The Bible gives factors that cause people to backslide. Some of these include shallowness (Luke 8:13), emptiness of life (Luke 11:24), worldly success (2 Chronicles 25:12), evil associations (1 Kings 11:4), lack of faith and understanding (John 6:63), the love of the world (2 Timothy 4:10), and even the absence of spiritual leadership (Exodus 32:1).

The temptation to become selfish also brings about backsliding, as brought out in Proverbs 14:14: "The faithless will be fully repaid for their ways." Religious indifference (Matthew 24:12), bondage to forms (Galatians 4:9-10), and reliance upon the sufficiency of the flesh or human effort instead of faith in God's spiritual power brings about backsliding (Galatians 3:1-4).

In the Lord's Prayer, Christ taught His disciples to be sensitive to the dangers of temptation. When Jesus gave the parable of the sower, He emphasized the importance of temptation in backsliding when He said, "Those on the rock are the ones who receive the word with joy when they hear it, but they have no root. *They believe for a while,* but in the time of testing they fall away" (Luke 8:13).

However, F. H., God is merciful, and when the backslider repents, believes, and is obedient, he is again restored to a blessed relationship with God. This happened to God's people when they had fallen away into sin. God promised, "I will heal their waywardness and love them freely" (Hosea 14:4).

$Q:$ **Why do people follow the crowd?—*B. A.***

$A:$ Your question is an important one because Jesus said, "Wide is the gate and broad is the road that leads to destruction, and many enter through it" (Matthew 7:13). Following the crowd is easy, but it is also very hazardous in both your spiritual and social life.

When you study the psychology of crowd behavior, you find that people feel there is "safety in numbers." This is believed for various reasons. One of the most obvious is that a person *loses his sense of responsibility* more in a crowd than alone.

Before the apostle Paul became a Christian, he took care of the coats of those in the crowd that stoned Stephen to death. Although he indirectly helped with the murder, he did not take direct responsibility. It was easy to appease his conscience by blaming the actual deed upon the crowd.

Some people follow the crowd because it is *difficult for them to make decisions alone.* Making decisions is not easy, and many people identify with a certain crowd and then adopt the will of the group. Psychological studies support the fact that the will can be weakened in a crowd. Beliefs and convictions are often cast aside if the resistance of the group is strong.

Many people follow the crowd because some of their *deepest needs are met* in the process. The needs for acceptance, popularity, and approval from others are satisfied when they identify with the crowd. People often conform quickly to the group so as not to be rejected. In fact, as a young person, B. A., you will find it very difficult to stand alone when the crowd differs with you.

Finally, there is usually *more emotion and excitement* in a crowd. Following the crowd can bring new experiences and thrills.

Nevertheless, if you are a Christian, you must remember that following Jesus is not always easy and popular. Jesus said, "Small is the gate and narrow the road that leads to life, and only a few find it" (Matthew 7:14). Don't let the crowd keep you from following Christ.

Q: **If you had to convert a person or give them an idea of Christianity in one minute, how would you do it?**—*G. C.*

A: This is an unusual question, G. C., but certainly a thought-provoking one. After receiving your question, I tried it on other young people like yourself to see what they would say. First let me give you a couple of responses and then state mine.

One young person said he would confront the other person with the question as to where he would spend eternity, and then introduce the concepts of fear and death. He would remind each person that everyone must die sooner or later, and it is an awesome question: "Where will you spend eternity?"

Some people object to using fear as a motive to convert people, but there is certainly a place for this approach. In the fifth chapter of the Acts of the Apostles when Ananias and Sapphira lied to the Holy Spirit and God caused their death, the 11th verse says, "Great fear seized the whole church and all who heard about these events."

One young person said she would spend her minute referring the person to the New Testament, particularly the Book of John. Certainly the Bible is the best source of reference to salvation and Christianity, but in one minute a person needs to be very specific in the quotations used.

For example, if you quoted John 3:16, you would quickly be emphasizing God's love, the universal scope of His salvation from sin, the sacrifice of Christ to provide for it, the importance of faith in receiving it, and the provision it makes for eternal life with God.

My approach would be that "All have sinned" (Romans 3:23), everyone needs forgiveness to have eternal salvation, and only Christ is the "way and the truth and the life" (John 14:6). Confession, repentance, and faith allow God to give His forgiveness and salvation from sin, and this brings peace and love between God and man.

DATE DUE

DEMCO 38-297